LIVE OUR LIES

Katie Noth

First published in Great Britain as a softback original in 2019

Copyright © Katie Noth

Typeset in Baskerville

Editing, design, typesetting and publishing by UK Book Publishing

www.ukbookpublishing.com

ISBN: 978-1-912183-74-6

"Don't let the bullies win."

LIVE OUR LIES

Katie Noth

Live our lies

Coming into the world, I was given the unfortunate short straw – a very embarrassing condition, known as congenital adrenal hyperplasia. Female babies born with this disorder have deformed, male-looking genitalia, making it hard to determine their gender. This was my case.

My story began with the marriage of two first cousins in the early 1950s, both of whom were already well on in life when I arrived. I was not welcomed into this world. My mother was horrid in the most heinous of ways – the first memory I have of her is me, a tiny baby in a cot, and her, pressing a pillow over my head, trying to suffocate me. As luck would have it, my father came into the room and put a stop to her, but she nearly succeeded. This trauma of my early childhood stayed with me for a long time afterwards – I was always afraid when she was near me, never trusting her temper.

My courtesy aunt, a long-time friend of my mother's, once received a letter from her, asking to arrange a meeting in Aberdeen's poshest restaurant. This being more of an order than a social occasion, she thought it was better to "do what she had been ordered to", get herself into some "glad rags", and get there when she'd been told to.

Aberdeen, at that time, was recovering from the Second World War. Bombings of the harbours and railway yards – especially Kittybrewster, or 'Kitty' – had left vast areas in rubble, like in most other cities that had come to the attention of the German War Machine. What people talked most about was the raider who had attacked Aberdeen. The deadly intruder had soon been noticed over the beach by Aberdeen's own squadron of fighters, who weren't going to let it go until they shot him down in flames over the city. The plane crashed into the middle of the Ice Rink. The loss of this entertainment venue seemed to really upset the Aberdonians – they never talked about anything else! Even in the 1960s, it was still a topic of conversation.

The restaurant was so posh, it had a quartet playing as you dined – now, that's style! They played their varying musical scores, surrounded by a wonderful array of pot plants: green leafy plants and exceptionally tall palm trees. Monty Don, eat your heart out! Hinge and Bracket must have taken a leaf from this well-established Edwardian *fossil* to get their act spruced up.

Before the meeting, my aunt was slightly apprehensive as the last time she'd frequented this establishment had been during the war. She and my mother had had a heated discussion on how the war was progressing. Much to her embarrassment, my mother had stood up in this genteel oasis of peace and opulence to declare that "the only good German was a dead one!" The embarrassment was mind-numbing. My aunt didn't know where to look, wishing the floor would open up for her to disappear into. This would have been a blessing. The looks and the atmosphere there were just awful after the dramatic forthright statement. Why they were never asked to leave, my aunt could not understand.

So there she sat, waiting in her Marlene Dietrich pose, cigarette in hand, puffing away, smoke wafting to the ceiling. Everybody did the same at the time, so the whole room was full of cigarette smog.

After some time, the nicotine fog gave way to reveal my mother, coming towards her. Her face was certainly not happy. After the formal pleasantries of meeting and ordering from the menu had finished, the small talk turned towards the real reason she had arranged the meeting – she needed advice on the best time to conceive. See, my mother was nearing 40 and her biological clock was ticking away. My aunt, by that time, had already had three children, and so my mother thought she was sort of an expert in the field.

Looking back on it now, the time my mother lived in could only be described as a very *unenlightened* age – the Dark Ages, really – as far as sex was concerned. As I was growing up, in the late 1960s, one time at school a female pupil was taken to the doctor's, complaining of movement in her stomach. When challenged by her mother and the doctor as to who the father of the soon-to-be-arriving child was, she claimed she had no idea. Only after some gentle encouragement, and a graphic account from the doctor of how babies were made, did she cough up the answer. The boy had snogged her for some time and when he got bored, knowing this girl was as dumb as they got when it came to sex, he suggested another way of 'kissing'. He showed her how. They got their kit off, and he did the 'kissing'. She was not to be too concerned if it was painful at first. It would soon pass, once she got the hang of it.

Who would believe this now? Rape by stealth! No other words for it. The times we lived in, which the youth now call 'retro', could never be understood in today's society. Even a mere mention of anything to do with the reproductive system got you into a no-go area. It sounds like a long time ago, but it wasn't, even though humanity has moved on and come up with so many brilliant, jaw-dropping inventions since then.

My mother and aunt began a deep intellectual conversation on the mysteries of the reproductive system, discussing a magazine article my dear aunt had read on this very subject. With the article still fresh in her memory, having read it only a few weeks before, she gave my mother the same advice. Note that the article had been written in a time when magazine content was of a much different nature than it is today. Some of the contemporary articles I see in women's magazines would have been classed as porn and would have never passed the censors; no-holds-barred columns, which I do not condone as educational, but hope that women are not taken in as they were in the past, and most importantly know what's right and wrong.

Armed with my aunt's knowledge, my mother went home to try out the article's recommendations. And they worked. She was pregnant. Normally, most women would find this to be a blessing, yet my aunt later received a very curt letter, requesting another meeting at the same venue. Somehow she knew it wasn't going to be pleasant.

She was there right on the button. The fizzing bomb was there all right. Thundering and raging, blaming her and the article for this predicament of a child on the way. The shock of the unexpected abuse and menacing attitude gave my aunt cause for concern for the wellbeing of this infant to come. My father assured her she would settle in time, saying it was just the surprise, and possibly fear, of the news. And he was partially right. During the rest of the time, before my arrival into this world, my mother was always right and faultless. But then I showed up and mucked it all up, this perfect utopia she had resided in. Having a child with a health condition had never been in her remit. I was rejected right there and then, and remained so with vigour until her death; sometimes the hatred diluted, but oh so very rarely.

Among all the goodwill cards I received on my birth, there was one unlike the others. It came in an especially dirty envelope, standing out from the rest. The card looked ordinary; however, the content was anything but: I received a poison pen letter, wishing me all the ill on this Earth with all the evil venom, blessed by the devil himself. The police were called in by the medics, who were shocked as to who could do such a thing. The handwriting was carefully analysed and studied, yet no culprit was found – they did have someone in mind but could not prove it. Now, sixty odd years later, it was a close relative of mine, I believe, who one day discussed the handwriting with me. I found the conversation quite disturbing and unsettling for a long time afterwards. It aroused my suspicions about the relative's hidden mean streak, which were fuelled by the most ancient of human frailties. Jealousy.

Such was my welcome into the world, where, I would say, the evil wished on me has been in bucket loads, surely pleasing this heinous author and fulfilling their life.

We lived in the outback of Aberdeenshire, in a glacier valley with gentle heather-covered slopes, ideal for sheep, of which we had hundreds. They were grey-faced and black-faced, good for rough grazing. I loved, and still do, all of the sheep, the sheep dogs, and most of the men who looked after them. To see hundreds of sheep waiting in the pens to be sheared was quite awe-inspiring. All were hand-sheared, at that time, by neighbours and other hang-abouts who were in various stages of, to put it politely, drink dependence. By the bottle, most of them battled demons they had fought in war – some in the Korean, some even in the Great War. But they were never to be spoken of. One man had had his ears so badly holed, they resembled pieces of expensive lace, hanging on each side of his head. Another one was a poor sod whose hand had been blown off, and they'd given him a rather natty, highly polished Captain Hook hook which, I think, was of no use for anything. One lovely lad once went for an X-ray; he got very angry, to put it mildly, with the lady who performed the procedure. She had told him to take off all jewellery and have no metal on him – being an Aberdeenshire farmer there was little fear of that. As he waited, he could hear a great confab going on outside, then the lady duly came back and said, "I thought I told you, Mr Gordon, to take off all jewellery and other metals." This set him off. He asked to see the X-rays, unable to understand what had made her think that. The lady came back with them and pointed out some sharp pointed items, one very close to his heart. Mr Gordon took one look at them, and told her he had been badly shot during the war. The medical chap later told him they would have to leave all the ordnance in him, as none of them could have been removed without causing damage to the vital organs around. The ordnance didn't bother him until the 1960s, but even then they still couldn't remove them. The ex-soldier has since told me of the field clearing station he had originally been taken to, of witnessing overwhelming casualties, and medics dead on their feet, coping in blind adversary.

I consider myself blessed and privileged for having met these men. They were old, some of them, but they still had a sparkle in their eye and the banter was good.

The village was established in the late XVIII century, with ongoing building developments happening to this day. One flaw of the town was it had one road, going in and out, thirty-six miles from habitation one way, and a good twenty-five miles the other; some small hamlets in-between, but nothing to speak of. Public transport was non-existent: one bus came in the morning, at some ungodly hour, and came back at an even stranger time in the evening. I now think that was the intention of the people in office at the time. Why, the village was full of every kind of depraved, perverted human known to mankind, so having no transport was one way of keeping occupants of the village in situ. The only other options were to either walk, since cars weren't common yet, or be picked up by the police at the bus stop, which happened much more often. No other escape from the County Alcatraz.

It was quite a prosperous village in its time. Victorian houses still on their own grounds, large gardens, two grocer's shops, a bakery, pub, shoe shop, the butcher's, a post office, the chemist's – which doubled as the bookies – garage, and of course, the ever-present police station, a church, a village hall, a school, a full-sized golf course, and a Chapel. The rot set in after the Second World War; some bright spark must have been travelling through this idyllic countryside. Guess, they realized how cut off it was from civilisation, and what a wonderful corralling point it would be for shipping problem families in by the wagon load. Out of sight, out of mind.

Houses were being built at breakneck speed. They looked so out of place in what had once been a lovely village. Today you would never get the permission to build these types of houses: out-of-context next to lovely, authentic Victorian homes.

The inhabitants of this country ghetto were the lowest of the low, picking up their livelihood at the post office; none of them actually worked, although they were good at working the system.

Soon, I would be propelled into this horrible howling-of-wolves type of school. Every child has the right to be safe where they are educated. To be taught by teachers who have the pupils' best interests at heart, who are there to give each child a chance to surprise themselves by what they can achieve. To inspire, to invigorate, the aim of the game. This is the fundamental right in education.

By this time, my mother had managed to put up with me, even trying to show me some care when it suited her, such as when people were around – it seemed to clip her venomous tongue, give me a rest from abuse. Otherwise, it would never cease. A good smacking just for good measure. When I was still an infant, she was particularly brutal. Twice she gave me a good beating. The first time, she got away with it; the second, my father caught her red-handed. Dear old Dad came in, stopped her with her hand mid-air. I'd always loved him, but I loved him even more for stopping her. She was furious for being caught.

Even our lovely sheep dog Bess did not like her. She always kept a watch on me, and an extra watch on my mother. She was a great part of my life, beautiful in all manners of her character – just like all Border Collies are. Bess would often come in from the fields to see if I was doing okay, poking me with her nose until I woke up. Then she would go back to doing her job as a sheep dog. Bess was my nanny.

Then there was another very special animal in my life that I could hug when everything was so black and black forever more – even a pin prick of light would have been a godsend. This delightful creature was a pony. A wonderful appaloosa, a spotted Dalmatian of the equine world, with a loving nature. She was just beautiful, full stop.

By then, I had already been primed for school. As per usual, I had a new school bag

and an all-new outfit to go to school in: a lovely
Gordon Tartan kilt, matching sweaters, a pair
of shoes… I wasn't going to a posh school but
a school which serviced the offspring of awful
people.

Mother and I set off for school. As I entered,
I found it full of children, chattering away in a
language I wasn't familiar with. It was known
as The Doric, a very ancient language, with
words dating back to the Pictish times – it's
not surprising it's still spoken to this day in the
hinterland of Aberdeenshire. Up until then,
I had been speaking Queen's English and
was proud of it, but my terrible apprehension
proved to be too well-founded to believe.

The school was run by a very tall
Headmaster, with a head of hair that any
'reggae' DJ would have been proud of. The
problem was, he had zero interest in his
pupils. In fact, he had zero interest in pretty
much anything. It was the pupils who ran the
school, as far as I could see, most of whom
were dangerous, out of control, and with
an unhealthy interest in seeing other pupils'
private parts. Today we call them perverts,
as they ticked all the boxes as to what we now

recognise in these types of people in modern day. They were very clever, hiding what they were doing, threatening violently, if need be. These children were snotty-nosed, ill-dressed, utter horrors. Even Steven Spielberg would have had a hard time, trying to replicate them in a film. Actually, there's not even a remote chance he could have.

First day at school is always traumatic, especially for a child who's been taken away from all she was familiar with, and thrust into a new life, completely alien. On our first day, we were given pencils, rubbers, and jotters, allocated a desk to sit at, and had explained to us the rules for break times… All such matters of school life that we're all so familiar with.

To be honest, my mother was quite kind to me when I started school. She told me about reading, writing and arithmetic, and had me well-versed on what was going to be taught. I was looking forward to it. I was always naturally curious about how things worked, and loved being read to. I highly treasured my picture books and longed to be able to read books with words cover to cover, often wondering what marvels could be gleaned from their pages. Once you can read, you become completely free in your mind and spirit.

Mother came to school for a few days to start me off. She wore the most beautiful red coat which I can still picture her in to this day. Seeing her go was terrifying. I knew something was wicked here, where I'd been left. She had instructed me to first trust my own head, then at all costs follow the older girls – whatever they told me to do, I'd better do it. In hindsight, it was the worst advice she could have ever given. Neither she nor I could have ever foreseen how perverted these children would be, this new ground that no child should have to cope with. It's different now, these things are talked about quite openly, perpetrators rightly hunted down, dealt with in court and declared as sex offenders, and then sentenced to life in prison with no remission. Justice can never be too severe.

My first memories of this Aberdeenshire school, are of all the boys running out the door at break time in a feverous riot, making bows and arrows, meant to be shot at the chimneys of the attached property, the Headmaster's house, with quite a number of them going straight down the target never to be seen again. Neither he nor his wife ever said a thing to them!

One boy from my school – who later started work at only fifteen – could not read nor write at the age of six. One time, he asked me if I would read to him and also teach him to sign his own name, which was long and laborious, since at the time I could hardly read and write myself. What I do remember, is how satisfying it was to be able to help him, how delighted his face was when he could finally sign his own name, and how much he enjoyed the few bits that I had read to him.

Then I met my own personal tormentors, dedicated to making my life miserable for the rest of my time in the Aberdeenshire educational system. Hell doesn't get a look in! I, like most civilised people, believe education is to be cherished. But there isn't a bit of it in this cut-off community, a completely alien environment to any decent human being.

One place every child must eventually go to in school is the toilet, a place where my ten-year nightmare began and later continued into the rest of my lifetime. This advice I got from my mother – to do what the older girls told me to – was what brought on the tragedy. I had never been warned of these sordid, heinous humans, nor did I know one. Neither did my parents, or my immediate family, or any of their friends. It was like being dumped into a cesspit, with no way out.

At age five, my life changed. One day some girls took me to the toilet and told me to do what they said, followed by the classic "Do NOT tell your mother or anyone else; it's forbidden". Backed up against one of the cubicles, I had to lift my lovely kilt. Finding that my knickers resembled an outer garment gave rise to a great discussion as to why I had a pair of knickers with a little pocket, which was usual for a flimsy pair of knickers. They were bottle green and very comfortable. The girls demanded to know why my mother would give me such a pair to wear. At five years old, you don't have much say, so you wear what you are given. Once they got over the shock of my green cherub knickers, they told me to take them down to my knees, revealing my liner pants. It once again confused them, causing quite a stir as to why I had on two pairs of knickers at the same time. I still recall the darkness of that day, the smell in the toilets, the lack of light in the cubicle… My next order was to take the other knickers down, too. This order, I thought, wasn't right, but I was so terrified that I did what they told me to, and took the knickers down. They all had a good look at my privates, shocked by the deformed vagina. These guttersnipes had just been given manna from heaven for their ruthless torture, humiliation and relentless ill-treatment. At one point, it got so bad you couldn't describe it on paper. No one would understand.

Within a split second, the whole school knew, and its pupils turned into fully-trained medics, though most of them weren't even six years old. The education that I had been told about and had looked so forward to was ruined the moment I walked in through the school door because of these horrible, dirty, inhumane creatures. And most of those girls, when they reached adulthood, went to work in healthcare, while others had careers in looking after old people and even children! I must admire the stealth of whoever employed them – they hadn't much of a Scooby.

It lasted for many years and I could no longer cope. Pleading with my parents to do something to stop at least some of the name-calling was of no avail – I just had to get on with it. So I became withdrawn, curled up in a quiet world of my own. But my small army of furry and feathered angels never let me down. The dogs, cats, bunnies, ponies and hens gave me love that never wavered. I would wrap my arms around these wonderful, blessed little creatures and cry my eyes out about what had been said to me. And they never told anyone! It was something I didn't want anyone to know about, not even my parents; I had to be brave at all costs.

Being a small child, sickly and withdrawn, gave my tormentors oxygen. Eventually, I stood up for myself. I asked one if he prayed before going to sleep in the hope he would have more horrible things to say to me. The next day, he stopped the name-calling, and he wasn't much of a problem anymore.

All my school work deteriorated. School reports came home with the customary 'US' scrawled all over – short for 'unsatisfactory'. This little yellow report card gave me the creeps to take home, along with a deep sense of foreboding. At least by now, I already knew a mouthful wasn't that much of a problem to cope with, compared to taking a beating. I've actually kept the worst one of those dreaded yellow report cards that I've ever taken home. I love to read it sometimes and remember the long, hard, unforgiving journey I've been on, which eventually brought me to my life here and now, full of wonderful people, laughter, and everything else that one needs to feel loved. Those girls – relentless.

The arrival of school holidays was total bliss. It was okay in the beginning, but time wore on and terror set in when I thought about going back to school and having to cope with the torment again. The only way I managed to cope was in hiding, where I would let my pain turn into buckets of tears, spilling over and streaming freely down my cheeks. Sometimes they just wouldn't stop.

The pickup point for the school bus was a local farm yard where a family of felons, who had committed quite a few crimes, were holed up. The 'greatest achievement' of this family was managing to put a local cattle dealer in jail for six months for a crime he never committed. Retribution for the framing came swiftly to the man responsible – his son was killed in a car crash before the cattle dealer was even out of prison. It was a topic of discussion for many years to come. Another son of the family had such a dislike for his father that he got himself an old, clapped-out car, filled it up with petrol, waited until he saw the poor old man out on the fields with no cover, then fired it up, slammed it into gear, and off he went, chasing his father through the fields. To escape the oncoming car, the old man barricaded himself in the farm buildings and remained there until they sorted out their differences. Such were these and numerous other tales that circulated about these wild people.

My involvement with these outlaw farmers was fairly minimal, apart from the turkeys. Hundreds of the huge, black, threatening birds were let out on the grass always just before I stepped off the school bus to walk home. These turkeys seemed much larger than me; they lived in droves and warned each other if anything strange happened. Once, they simply glanced at me, and one of them called out in alarm, giving rise to total pandemonium as they'd decided to get me off the property, pronto. Having been quickly surrounded by these larger-than-life birds, I made for the closest fence, and got through it to safety.

By Christmas time and New Year, sadly, the turkeys had had it. As a result, I could vault or crawl under any fence set in front of me. Winters are so much milder now. No modern-day person could really understand the intense cold and the bitter winds, the deep snows and the legendary snow storms of Aberdeenshire, as well as in Upper and Lower Banffshire. These suffocating storms have killed and maimed numerous men, women and children – the beast spared nothing and no one in its fury. Storms would blow for days. Outer farmsteads, in particular, would choke with the lying and drifting snow. Man and beast, all were inside, sheltered from the Arctic blasts of our worst storms that came from the North-East coast, but originated in the steppes of Russia.

One family once opened their front door to find themselves trapped in the farm house – the snow had blocked all doors and windows. Luckily, one of them had taken shovels in the night before as the storm only began to rage the next morning. They tried to shovel the snow into the kitchen, the living room, and eventually the hallway, but, becoming rather frightened by the amount of snow that had already accumulated, they stopped to discuss what the next best move would be. Finding not even the faintest glimmer of hope to get nearer to the surface, they decided to start shovelling again, this time out of the kitchen to make space to heat up some food. Suddenly, the lady of the house had the lightbulb moment: they went into the attic with a step ladder to try the skylight, which turned out to be freer of snow as a slight tinge of light could be seen, but it had frozen shut. So they melted the snow, boiled it, used bottles filled with hot water, and somehow finally managed to free the skylight and stick their heads out to inspect the panorama. The view was breath-taking, with feet of snow, stretching for infinity. They were one of very few families that were so well-prepared; they managed to slip out through the skylight and use it as their new front door for the rest of those snowy months.

The roads were completely impassable, despite all the usual preparations that had been made: miles of snow fences were sometimes put up three feet deep at notorious places where drifting snow was to be expected, along the snow poles which kept everybody aware of where the road was supposed to be. Eventually, the County Council shipped in snow blowers from Canada and Norway to clear the roads; one village had to be reached by going through a tunnel of snow. These snow blowers were so novel, most of the population came out to see them in use, blowing great showers of snow off the roads, leaving behind these amazing cuttings. Frozen vistas with hard frost, it wasn't all doom and gloom. Even though it lasted for several months, people knew how to drive, so getting around wasn't a problem. Chains on tyres and other preparations were crucial for these winters; in the unfortunate event that you got stuck, there was always a humble shovel with a bag of sand – a standard kit – in the boot. But there was always help available, too – very rarely did people pass someone stuck on the road. Once, we stopped to push a dear neighbour in his nice new car up the gradient, where a post van had come around the corner and hit the front of his car. After insurances had been exchanged, we decided to turn the now not so new-looking car towards the garage some miles away. Unfortunately, another car showed up and, giving the gradient a good bit of welly, hit this car square in the front, which was very unfortunate for both parties. The car now looked as though it belonged in a scrap yard. We gave our condolences to the new car in its sorry state: headlights and tail-lights were hanging off, and some other bits were deeply bent. We left, then, as it was still road worthy enough to get to the garage.

Another story of how heart-rending hard frost can be has even made it into newspapers. Some neighbours spotted a flotilla of yellow bath ducks, bobbing half-way up a panorama window of a very expensive bungalow, and called the police. They had a hard time persuading the plod to come with a key to turn off the water or get someone to turn off the water. Eventually, the officer found out that these people had been on holiday and weren't returning for another two weeks, but no one knew where they'd gone and so couldn't contact them. The police, once they got their act together, were very good, got someone to turn off the water supply outside, then came back to see the owners, after they had returned, to help them recover from the shock of their home being completely destroyed.

These storms were a godsend to me, though – I didn't have to face my horrible, disgusting classmates. Sometimes we were sent home mid-day or didn't go to school at all – the weather was so awful. Often, in times of such severe snow, the sun would be out and, if you were sheltered, the warmth of the sun made it look more like a chocolate box Swiss scene rather than a Scottish one. To be complacent in these weather conditions, in some instances, proved to be fatal. Just thinking you could beat this kind of weather was dicing with death. And death often won. Two school children once suffocated on their way home, one just steps from the safety of their own home. So heart-breaking for their parents and siblings…

The tragic experience of chilly winds and drifting snow made the educational authorities more likely to send children home if similar weather was expected. One time, the school closed because of a drifting snow forecast, but it turned out to be a cheat as the sun was out with a horizon-to-horizon bright blue sky. It was also warm when I was walking home, but you didn't need a degree in weather forecasting to know something awful was brewing.

My welcome home to safety wasn't delightful that day. As soon as my mother set eyes on me, she went into a rage, telling me that I had walked out of school and come home under my own steam, and I had to go back at once. I tried to explain to her why the whole school had been sent home – because of the drifting snow – but it only seemed to make her rage even more. She got so furious, she went and phoned the Headmaster, demanding he explain why I was at home and not at school, to which he gave the same reason as I had a few minutes earlier. Eventually, he told her that if I was to be taken back, there would be no teaching staff or pupils, and that she should be glad that I was home, indoors and safe, as the rest of the children were. But she still wasn't satisfied with the Headmaster's reasons for closing the school, and so went on to phone the school bus staff to see how the roads were. They told her the same thing – to stay inside and to be glad that I had been sent home! The roads were nearly completely impassable by now, and they were waiting for a snow plough to arrive and clear the road so that one of their drivers could get home in his bus.

By this time, my father had come in to ask if she would heat up some soup and hot tea with milk and sugar, and fill a few flasks with them. Every flask we had in the house was filled and taken to the people stuck in the drifting snow by his men, who were also ordered to try and clear some traffic, if possible. They did the best they could with these conditions that the rather bedraggled travellers found themselves in, but eventually, the police had to organise the snow plough to come and clear the road, letting the people at least get to the village, where they could be put up for the night until the weather settled down. But when it did settle, the drifts were herculean and all roads were shut for a few days, until the snow blowers got their teeth into the white, powdery snow and roads were finally cleared. Or at least until the next blast from the Arctic or the steppes of Russia.

My take-out from all of this drama was manna from heaven – I couldn't attend school for a week. A treasured time, so precious to me, it gave me some rest from the unending terrors of school life. Every second away from that place was a gift. Anything that kept me away from school was to be worshiped, then held in holy reverence.

I had an extra bonus, when one storm brought drifts all around the farm steadings. I couldn't resist sledging on these wonderful drifts. It was great fun, until I came down with the flu, which then turned into pneumonia. Now this one was serious – I had to be off-school for some time. I don't remember much as I slept most of the time, but I do remember the fires my mother lit and kept going – nobody had central heating then, so open fires were the norm – and a radio broadcaster once reading a story about a black cat that scared me half to death. Being in this delirious state, I watched the furniture grow larger and larger, then recede just as quickly. I found out, years later, it was called Alice in Wonderland syndrome, which is a fancy term for being very ill, with the brain playing tricks when you're highly feverish. Eventually, I started to get better, which meant that the day I'd dreaded for so long – when I would have to go back to the living hell – was fast approaching.

There were still mountains of snow at the pickup point at the end of the road, where I waited with the other children for our school bus. Marvellous, steel-hard cuttings of snow everywhere; the amazing heaps were quite awe-inspiring. Telephone lines were also somewhere in these roadside heaps. We went to look for them. Digging in the snow, we found the wires were well below the surface. So we balanced along them, just to say we had done it, once the wires begin to appear again.

These children were two girls and one boy. The oldest girl, for sure, lived to give me hell. Her father was a commander, but he never spoke of the war. The girl used to tease me, saying my father would be dead soon, since he was older than hers. Her words stressed me out so much, it would often have me in tears. But then their father died unexpectedly, without any warning – his body was found where he'd gone to repair some fences. There was no laughing after that.

This girl also found pleasure in running around me, with her hands in the air, singing "I'm perfect, you're not". She tried to goad me, staring into my eyes, but I never said anything, telling myself I was better than that. A time came when, still a teenager, she fell pregnant. The very sad thing was, her baby's brain was damaged: she couldn't see, speak or be fed. The infant lived for a couple of years and died quietly in her sleep, which, considering the difficult start to her life, was a blessing. Needless to say, she never taunted nor ran around me with her jibes ever again. I never said anything to her about the child, though. I just let it lie.

The other girl, her younger sister, cried 'rape' after attending a local village disco, pointing her finger at the son of the local outlaws. She had no idea of the repercussions of such an accusation – police interest, the court, the newspapers and press, all way beyond her imagination. In those times, medical testing wasn't possible, as it is now, to determine whether the accused was guilty of rape or not. The men were completely at the mercy of the accuser – now times have changed, thankfully. The family drove forty miles to the court with their daughter only to see her get into the witness box, swear an oath to tell the truth, then announce the boy hadn't done it! The press had a field day, plastering the story all over the front page no less. Whatever happened after the village disco, she denied he had ever touched her. This must have been very annoying and embarrassing for the parents and siblings alike.

Both sisters packed their bags to leave for the land of Sheila, never to be heard of again. As for the outlaws' son, I remember seeing him with the school halfwit's knickers on the ground, backed up behind a tree in a very public area – the school playground – he, the ring leader of the other boys having a good eyeful.

The school was perverts' heaven on Earth, but the weird thing is, the villagers were all mostly the same low-life. One farmer often told the tale of when he decided to walk his sheep through the village to new pastures. Not being a local man, coming quite a distance, he was a new face to the villagers, who watched him as he herded his flock with his faithful sheep dogs, making him very uneasy. But I know this man was no coward – he'd fought in the First World War and had been in the Gordon Highlanders for three years. These men were no push-overs; Devils in Skirts, the enemy called them.

He settled his flock into the new pastures, secured the gate and turned to go home on foot with his dogs. When he approached the village again, this time he noticed more of a crowd waiting for him. This really unsettled him – which wasn't easy to do as he'd fought in some of the most withering of battles – in the Great War – and his premonition was right. It wasn't something he could have thought of; he was a decent man. This poor soul was grabbed, then stripped of his trousers and underwear, his genitals given a good look-over by this disgusting horde of young and old, male and female, even children were in the mix. The sexual assault took place in broad daylight, just around a corner where this terrifying horde would stand, come rain or shine.

Before the arrival of television, radio or everything else we know of today, large groups of people like this one stood on street corners and in shop doorways. Owners of these properties had to place iron spikes on their windowsills to keep these hang-abouts off. It was the norm in the North East of Scotland's villages to hang about in droves, but not to this extent. They were a one-off.

Needless to say, the farmer never set foot in the village ever again. Instead, he sent transport to take his sheep home at the end of the pasture season, telling the driver not to stop in the village, at any cost. The ordeal had traumatised him, and his wife and family could not get to grips with what kind of people would do this to him and why.

My own experience wasn't any better in the hands of these people. They were disgusting, vile to the core. They destroyed others' lives; some had to attend a night school, once they left school, to get the grades needed to get on in life. Not one of these poor pupils went to college or university, which was a total disgrace and reflected badly on the teachers working at the school.

After those girls had forced me to take my pants down in the school toilets and threatened me not to tell anyone, especially my parents, life became a living hell. Now, I cannot urge you enough to speak out if anything untoward has been asked of you or done to you. You **must** talk to someone. Once you do, the grip of these people will diminish, and their power over you will fall to zero.

I didn't, and that's where it all went wrong. I kept their dirty secret to myself, I didn't tell. Being a small child, how could I? These children were frightening at the best of times. I often say that the school was a good old-fashioned borstal in all but the name; the pupils were dangerous, to say the least. And it wasn't just me, I found out much later, who was so frightened of them. Others have told me how they had to attend a night school to complete their studies, just to get the basics of their education which they'd been denied by these horrors. Decent children were ruthlessly targeted, no mercy shown.

Once they saw I had this carbuncle on my front bum, I got called all sorts of names, but mostly that I was a boy. They were treating me like I had leprosy, cleaning their hands off my clothes, making sure they hadn't caught anything from me.

As a child, the school toilets were a place of fear for me and dread. Once, I wet myself on the classroom floor because I couldn't bring myself to ask to go to the toilet, as one of these horrors would have surely been told to take me there, then assaulted me. I was in no doubt of it. These types of children were very cunning, threatening and frightening from an early age.

One time, I found this very handsome caterpillar, climbing up the stairs of the school. I had no idea how it got there or why it was crawling up those stairs. Being interested in all things nature, I sat down to look at it. It was one of those with all the hair on it.

There were also children of prisoners of war (**POW**) going to my school. Their fathers could not return to their homeland, which had been overrun by the Red Army, so they stayed there and married Scottish girls, eventually starting a family. Some never lost the Nazi doctrine and still believed they were the master race by all accounts.

One son of the POWs came over to me, saying he also wanted to watch the caterpillar, and sat down on the other side. A girl he played with at times – they were neighbours of sorts – joined us, wanting to watch the caterpillar, too. What they really came there to do, however, was to grab both my arms at either side, so I could do nothing to defend myself, and pull my knickers down to my knees. Then they laughed and laughed. To be exposed like this was degrading and humiliating, to say the least.

But the old saying 'what you sow, you shall reap' held true some years later, when the boy went to sea as a fisherman. On his first trip out to the fisheries, the others noticed he'd gone missing from the deck of the trawler. They looked around, but there was no sign of him, until one of the crew members noticed him miles behind the trawler, entangled in the nets, disappearing under the waves. When they hauled back the nets, they found him dead. He'd drowned, of course. His ample head of hair was wrapped round the fishing gear – a gale had been blowing his hair, it got caught in the main wire of the nets, he'd gone overboard with the net, and that was that. I wonder what he thought of as he went to his doom.

The girl, years later, found herself working as a housekeeper and a cook for a wealthy farmer in the middle of Aberdeenshire. When she opened the door to let me in – I had to stay for some afternoon tea with this chap – her face went red. As she came in with tea cakes, everything was shaking uncontrollably on the tray. Her face was beetroot-red. It was a sight to behold and it gave me great satisfaction, but I didn't say a word.

The stairs is a nightmare soft spot for anything untoward to happen – you need your balance to manage on the steps. One boy from a family of three, who in modern day would be classed as a problem child, took it upon himself to try and shove me down the stairs, and he nearly succeeded. He shoved me in the back, and losing my step, I hung on to the banister for grim life. The stairs were built of concrete with metal edging, and it would have given me a severe injury, if he'd achieved his goal, but I denied him that pleasure. The next time he tried that again, I made sure he was in front. I just couldn't understand the mentality of this boy, and his siblings were just as bad, if not worse.

After being frightened on the stairs, I became much more astute – dare I say, wily – even at that young age. Anything to preserve my life and limb. These children were very dangerous – there was no getting away from that.

My next delight from this 'no-fun' child, was to be snowballed with hard ice snowballs – his inspiration came from a teacher who once gave a lesson on how dangerous and grave the consequences of being hit on the head with an ice snowball or hard snow could be for one's eyesight. When she had been younger, she had had one such experience resulting in a partial loss of eyesight, firing up this *arsehole's* imagination no end.

On the playground, I have dodged a hail of hard ice snowballs better than any he could make, aim, and throw. Overnight, some divine intervention prevailed, melting all the snow and therefore stopping his hideous game.

This *arsehole* was a special one, right out of the devil's brew. He had it in for me; killing myself was his dream. Sometime later, I had to go in for surgery for a quite difficult procedure – I had to have two of my ribs removed initially, then the offending bit, too. It took me a fortnight of being really ill before finally getting back on my feet and returning to school. Lining up at the bottom of the dreaded stairs to go to classes, there was that *arsehole* barnacle in my face again, asking why I'd had been away. Within a split second, I was on the floor, him kicking me in my still raw wound without any mercy, telling me that they'd thought they'd got rid of me this time, and that next time I shouldn't come back. A teacher pulled him off me and gave him a dressing-down. It helped, as he didn't bother me so much after. He found his 'dream job' as a doorman of this nightclub company. In one of their venues, the door staff have later been charged with a terrible mistreatment of punters, when they stepped out of line. Surprisingly, this *arsehole* wasn't featured in the newspaper report; he could have mended his ways by some miracle.

The stairwell was a place of nightmares that not one person of authority ventured into. In fact, nobody would in their right mind. Those horrors all congregated in a mass in this area at break time. The noise was so deafening. They were obviously out of control, akin to the *Lord of the Flies;* not one adult came to restore sanity in the place, completely bereft of discipline.

The school planning was such that the stairwell led to an inner emergency exit door, which then led to a dark space, akin to a large box room, furnished with an old-fashioned radiator and a very large coconut carpet to clean your feet on, and then to the main outer door into the playground. In the confined space lurked the cauldron of pervert boys, mostly, pulling any girl into it, throwing her down on the coconut carpet, ripping her knickers down to expose her privates to the world. This happened time and time again, and the only way these horrors stopped was by moving on to something worse. One of the culprits exposed himself in the classroom regularly, when the teacher wasn't around. His willy was more out of his trousers than in. Disgracing every decent man on Earth, this heinous monster should have been jailed, never to see the light of day again, and put on the sex offenders list for life, along with the others. But instead, he hid himself away by joining the ancient order of plods – how that happened is beyond me or anyone else to understand.

Becoming wily, indeed, I would head out through doors we weren't supposed to use. I had been adhering to the rules, while being sexually assaulted by these disgusting horrors. They'd caused enough embarrassment and shattered my confidence, humiliating me at every opportunity, leaving me with a very low self-esteem. Not knowing the words for private, taboo body parts hindered my ability to tell someone about what was going on – not that anyone in authority would have believed me, anyway.

The large box room, the hallway, held nightmares for me of another kind. When it wasn't inhabited by the other horrors, in here lurked the so called 'big girls'. These tyrants, in every possible colour, barely out of infancy, could get every accolade for terrorising and physically harming the pupils with ruthless, sustained efficacy. It never relented – whether it was spring, summer, autumn or winter – not once during the whole ten years that I attended the school.

These girls demanded access to our family home, wanting to look around our farmhouse, arriving in all their glory, with their snotty noses pointed, walking nearly two miles from the village, down the rough track to our home on a cold, wet evening. Anyone else would have been glad to stay inside in the warmth, but these were determined, wanton bullies, who forced entry into our family home. Nobody had invited them anywhere near the place; they were so threatening that I thought it was best to give in and let them come, to get them out the door as soon as possible – right where they belonged.

They did try my mother's lipstick, which didn't set my mother off as it usually did. She never said anything, not a thing, to these girls, who were obviously so far from normal. They came and they went, leaving me feeling like there had been a vicious personal assault on both my family and my home, although it used no violence, just terror.

Completely bereft of the slightest flicker of conscience, they would sadistically pull my hair, make me kiss their feet, then do the Ring a Ring a Rose around me, singing about how my privates were deformed.

Soon, the school was absorbed into another school for some time to let the council upgrade the school. A public meeting was held, during which a local dignitary stood up beside the Headmaster, telling the assembled audience and sundry they didn't need an upgrade, but a new Headmaster, because this one beside him was utterly and totally useless, in every sense of the word. But the Headmaster soldiered on for what seemed like forever.

Travelling, during the merger of the two schools, was just awful; I had to change from one bus to another, instead of taking just one like I used to. The government had recently decided to use European time, so it was dark in the morning and dark in the afternoon. It was terrible – your body never got the rest it needed during winter.

In the new school, these horrors were much more diluted in their viciousness, since they knew the Headmistress wasn't as tolerant to abuse as ours. At least, they were… until they had her all figured out and knew just how to get away with things without being punished. From then on, there was no rest for me; the abuse was unending.

My father owned numerous shotguns and rifles, and used them to keep vermin in check on the farm. Unlike today, you could have all sorts of weaponry without much fuss. Now this would never be allowed; if you tried to even have anything like the arsenal we had, you would be in prison in the blink of an eye. But it wasn't just us – every farm had their own selection of ammunition.

From an early age, I could strip and clean Dad's weapons. Later, he also taught me how to shoot. One day, I just couldn't stand any more of these horrors. I sat there for a long time, with the rifle loaded, wondering if I could just end it. All I managed to do was to put the muzzle to my temple, before I realized: if I pulled this trigger, the vile horrors would win. A very strange thing happened the next day at school, and for some time that followed – they didn't bother me so much anymore. As if I'd been given the strength to cope with them by some guardian angel, or this angel had started to protect me.

But the relief from torture didn't last very long, as I was later allocated a seat beside this girl, at a double Victorian desk. These types of desks were made of oak and were very heavy; they could have withstood a direct hit from a bomb, if need be. They had folding up seats, steel tubing for legs, and a sharing space for books, even museum pieces, underneath the desk. And it was this space that later became an Achilles' heel for me. It really needed a special type of person to dream up the kind of things they said I was doing under the desk, in front of the teacher, in front of the whole class. They had very filthy, perverted minds, these children. Apparently, I had been *kissing* the girl under the desk. I did – and I shall admit it full-heartedly – laugh with her sometimes, under the desk, but I never did anything they blamed me for.

Next, they organised for me to be sent to Coventry where not a single soul would speak

to me for a long time – weeks, even. It had a
very detrimental effect on me mentally. Think
about how awful I felt.

Being slightly dyslexic, I found I could do
Maths better if I used my fingers to count.
It helped enormously with the lessons on
arithmetic, but at the same time, it gave
one *arsehole* the oxygen of a braying donkey
to ridicule every bit of effort that I put into
Maths. Once, I managed to top the class, and
the boy threatened me to not do that again,
or he, that little *shit*, would give me a good
going-over. But who cares – I learnt to count,
despite these despicable *arseholes*.

By the end of term, these pupils were just
too much for anybody to handle. My parents
weren't very helpful, saying I should just get
on with it. Even when I pleaded with them,
they thought I was being soft and that I could
handle it. Well, I couldn't handle it anymore.
An opportunity arose to get shot of these
pupils for some time, which I grabbed onto
with both my hands, as any sensible person
would have. I managed to convince my
parents that I should repeat the year, as I had
fallen behind quite a bit because of the illness.

I was at that point now where I just didn't care whether I would miss out on moving forwards with my education. All I wanted was to get shot of these pupils, who were getting more violent and difficult to control. I wished to have nothing to do with them.

In the end, the wish was granted. I felt such relief for the time being, knowing it would be short-lived and therefore savouring every moment. Not having them at me all the time, being able to run around and laugh – something every child should be allowed to do – was marvellous. This one thing was what gave lift to my spirits.

Because I was so focused on them being out of my life, it took me a long time to realise that my school work had also improved and seemed easier overall. Gone were the days of them cleaning their hands on me, gone were horrible pupils who pulled my knickers down whenever they could. Twice I'd had to endure depraved perverts doing that. One pupil wore very thick prescription glasses for reading as a result of a brain tumour or something, but it didn't stop her being devious. She tried to get me to hold them once, but I refused, so she had arranged for this other pupil to bump into me, try to have me drop them so my parents would have to pay for breakages and all that it would endlessly entail.

That girl from hell had two brothers. They, too, were two nasty bits of work. They got away with everything until the day they were at work and tried their ways there. They were soon lifted by the police, convicted and sentenced to be birched. They were given a set number of strokes which seemed to be enough as they were weeping, racked in utter pain, for hours. After the deed had been done, no one ever heard of them again. Later in life, when I spoke of birching with other people – none had ever met or known anyone that had been birched.

The teacher wasn't all sweetness and light. She was a brutal, hard lady. I remember being very badly shaken by her. My crime was not writing down Roman numerals correctly – even though I did. Being left-handed, I wrote them backwards, towards the front. The teacher furiously shook me for this, until she realised I had all the numerals, but the wrong way round, and that it was because I was left-handed. She then eased off on me.

Left-handed people have also been found to be very artistic. Once in school, we had to mix different colours of paint to get another colour. The task was simple for me, always having had paint boxes and crayons and pencils around. Purple was the colour we needed to come up with in that morning's lesson. So I mixed up the colour purple, as told, and the teacher went around everybody, not saying a word. But then she came to me and completely lost her temper, all in a second. Why? Because I had a better colour than the rest. She grilled me stupid on how I'd managed to mix this colour, until I asked if I hadn't heard her right and if it was some other colour that we needed to mix up. She seemed to come to her senses and stop as quickly as she had flared up.

She also picked on me when I wasn't able to spell something. This was ridiculed in a very savage way, and then I realised she was out to get me. I could see from her body language and her 'Don the Dunces' cap'. She was sitting on a stool in the front of the class. It was like feeding the piranhas; my payback for daring to mix the paint better than the rest. I am dyslexic like many others, get along just like the others, and I cause no trouble. But at the time, dyslexia wasn't a very well-known condition, and you were just left to be misunderstood and mocked.

One time, she did show me mercy and compassion, though. I had just come back to school after a cold or something, having been off for some time. I was sitting in the classroom, looking at the clock, as it was getting near three in the afternoon. I looked round at all my awful classmates. I couldn't help the tears that began to well up and run down my cheeks in huge droplets. At three in the afternoon my mum would feed our hens and would take me with her. I loved it; the hens all gathered round, picking up the grain she had scattered, chattering amongst themselves. They were such *chatters*! And while they had their great conversations with each other, we would collect the eggs.

So I sat there, thinking of our chatty hens and egg collecting, surrounded by my classmates. Two of them committed murder later in life, with no evidence to convict;

another turned into a rapist, elderly ladies being his speciality; a fraudster, picked up at an airport by the police and given some sort of sentence; another one killed a female passenger in his car by speeding, and it made no difference to him. All of them were wily, sly and cunning.

Not having my hens and other animals with me set the tears in motion. I could not believe the uncontrollable amount, rolling down my face. I wept for such a long time, feeling depressed, frightened and homesick. The teacher had some sympathy for me that day – I commend her for the little of it that she showed.

There was also a boy in my class who once urinated in another boy's shoe. Another time, he threw a knife into a spanking new blackboard – one of the rolling ones that are not used anymore, taken out of packaging a day before he destroyed it, moments after being left by himself in the classroom. Yet another time, on a school trip to the seaside, he and his brothers went hot-foot to buy fishing hooks, a line and bread to feed the seagulls, then catch them and just laugh. He did get in trouble for that.

Not one of these pupils went to college or university to get themselves into jobs where they would be left in charge of vulnerable people and who would be their priority. No need to wonder why.

As time wore on in the new school, the Aberdeenshire village had more going on and wasn't cut off nor in the backwater of Aberdeenshire, which made it more pleasant. They now had a new Headmaster, a very short man, who fancied himself as God's gift to women. One day, he arrived, kitted out in the military uniform of a major, swagger stick under his arm, paraded around school before setting off to war games, courtesy of NATO, as a reservist.

A new interest at the school caused him a severe problem, leaving him quite puzzled as to how it could be cracked – Albert Einstein would have told him it was a difficult one. The problem was that he just couldn't get the new Deputy Headmistress, who had just arrived, a blonde bombshell, to part with her knickers. She just wouldn't drop them.

He kept trying – our legend of King Robert, the Bruce's spider in the cave, burned onto his brain. Tried and tried again; eventually succeeded. The knicker elastic sprung, his trophies included sex in the staff room, up the back of the door, the staff room floor, on the sofa, on the table, up the walls, the broom cupboard, the janitor's cupboard. The dear old secretary had forms to be signed. Hearing moaning and groaning coming from his office, she knocked intrepidly on the door. He got himself pulled together with relative decency; no sign of the nymphomaniac, only a pair of knickers, lying a foot from his desk. Perfect hands and nails came out from under his desk, trying to retrieve the undergarment, but with little success. Quick-thinking, this delightful old lady kicked the offensive knickers towards the hand, helping her to retrieve them. Seeing them disappear under the desk was a relief to both parties. The 60s' Carry On film didn't come close. In the meantime, in the real world, his wife went on producing babies with the regularity of a well-oiled sausage machine on high octane steroids.

The Headmaster would always take the unruly pupils to task – this man really deserves a gold star for how he tried to be a stickler. Punishments could still be meted out in bucket loads in the form of a very thick, eighteen inches long leather strap, thongs cut into its end to make it more *pain-efficient*. It was a relic of the Victorian educational system, the slave trade, and the royal navy. It taught obedience and discipline just fine, until you had someone who enjoyed the power of it to the extreme, and then it wasn't funny anymore. But it was unlikely that aging would improve the ingrained behaviour of these horrors. Even staff were so shocked by their frightening and dangerous attitude towards them. I realised, at some point, the endgame of schooling. At last, a pin prick of light on the horizon. I now looked forward to better times, without these creatures blighting every aspect of my life.

The *original* pupils – those who were in this school before we arrived – attending the catchment area of the school, wondered what had crashed in on them. They weren't in that same league whatsoever; they were lovely, smart pupils, who wanted to go far in life. And they did just that, working hard on their studies to pass exams and all. The rough new element – the horrors that arrived from my school – toxic as ever, plied their trade with marked vengeance, ruthless and efficient. The perverts were back in their element, looking at all the new-to-them girls' privates, accomplishing this *delight* by taking them one by one into the toilets, pulling their pants down, threatening them not to tell their parents, just like they had done to me. The ring leader of this group later spent her life caring for the elderly in a sheltered housing complex, in the village where she grew up in. I always felt so sorry for the residents having to be looked after by that awful woman. Everybody wondered why the service company had employed her. It was yet another of those mysteries.

The perverts also tried it with my new friend I'd met at this school. Having none of it, she had to literally fight them off when she went to the toilets, but unlike the other girls, she spoke out about it time and time again, long after leaving. Her loving parents made an appointment with the Headmaster to discuss these pupils and what could be done with the intention of having them expelled. But they immediately hit a brick wall. Nothing they pleaded with or said to convince this man moved him into action. Instead, they got nothing but horseplay and a right load of *bullshit* about how their daughter shouldn't take life so seriously.

As a parent, you always wish your child the fairest chance in life, along with the best educational grounding. So the Headmaster's sweep-it-under-the-carpet attitude left her mother grief-stricken and her father livid with rage, as his reply was what no parent wanted to hear. In the end, their daughter transferred to a night school to get her grades, and she did very well.

The next incident at the school cost a family the father's job – he was a gardener at a lovely large country house with grounds, which he kept in pristine condition – and their home, which was a tied house. Their little boy had a birthday party, which some of the children were invited to as you would normally do. Sensibly, they didn't invite those unruly pupils. Who, in their right mind, would have them in their house? Madness, if they had. As a result, these utterly awful pupils thought up a punishment for this lovely little child – they burned his hands on scalding-hot water pipes that were taking heat round the school. The boy went home and showed his parents the scalded hands. His father went to see the Headmaster. Again, a brick wall; he said they had already been punished, and that was that. The boy never came back to school; his parents left the area within a week. Presumably, finding a job for his father was easy as he was a very good gardener, but he wasn't putting up with what had been done to his son.

My next run-in with the school's perverted rabbit boiler became nearly fatal at a game of hockey on a lovely, sunny, warm afternoon. The rules of hockey had been explained to all of us, but the P.T. teacher wasn't with it that these pupils had their own rules. We started the game and my team was winning, until this pupil raised her stick up over her shoulders – which isn't allowed by the rules – and the stick caught me on my throat, closing the wind pipe and leaving me gasping for air for a long time. In fact, I thought I wasn't going to live. I could see everybody whirling round me, until my windpipe opened and I could breathe again. In the meantime, the culprit stood on the playing field, shouting that I shouldn't have been there – but I was, because it was a game of hockey, and it was her who didn't play by the rules. The P.T. teacher just looked guilty whenever he saw me, since he never said a thing to this girl. He didn't even remind her of the rules of the game.

Realizing that I had nearly lost my life to a game of hockey made me more astute at just how you can be here one minute and gone the next, through no fault of your own. I still love watching hockey, though! Especially ice hockey, which is great entertainment, good fun and they adhere to the rules.

My love of art and making things was my solace and saviour. Apart from being arty-crafty-minded, I also had great teachers who enthused and stimulated me. The unruly classmates would usually leave me alone at these classes, except for one time when they dripped paint all over my nearly-completed work. It really upset me, as I'd done quite a nice woven runner, and the pupils rendered it useless, through mindless spite. The loom came from a dear great aunt of mine. Our Art teacher would set the loom up. We both found the instructions confusing – some bits of the loom didn't even fit – but we didn't mind, as long as it did the job. I never used it again after the paint had been thrown over the work.

Many of these classmates died in their twenties because of illness, accidents and other mishaps. Maybe they had succumbed to the curse associated with congenital adrenal hyperplasia? It is well known that those who treat people with this condition well get on in life, having great luck. Others fall foul of the curse. I pity those who do; it usually means death or something else so bad, it makes you clutch your pearls.

All of these dark, absolutely lightless years never gave me any hope of improvement. My confidence was at a total zero; educational achievement less than desired. And it wasn't just me. Those horrors destroyed the lives of many others, but no one said anything to them. They were untouchable, in every sense of the word.

Reading books was my saviour; finding out I wasn't so dumb gave a great boost to my ego. Having amazing people, who seemed to fall into my lap out of nowhere, added up to the great social circle I've gathered, showing how having beautiful people around can help you withstand the snotty noses. The ones that are just so plain pug-ugly.

When I left school, I couldn't stop crying with utter joy. My mother wondered what was wrong, but it was just outright joy gone off the rails. I often wish I could say something nice about those classmates, but after suffering them for years, it would all be lies.

In time, a lovely new couple came to the practice as the new doctors. They were really on the ball and shook things up in no time. They took an interest in my condition and soon referred me away from this awful man I had previously seen. Also, after refusing to set foot back in his department, I went to another chap and was supposed to have surgery soon to correct my bum. The dire man was found to be an alcoholic and deeply hated by other medical staff for the way he treated his patients. I cannot thank the new doctors enough for their kindness. It was like stepping out of hell and into heaven.

My grandmother buried two of her sons before she too passed away: one as an infant, another through being exhausted after the war. You would never have known of her suffering, though, she always encouraged all of her grandchildren, not just me, to read and read, to educate myself through all types of books.

My love of cooking has been passed down to me by my awful mother, but also my two lovely grandmothers. With time and a few false starts, I managed to hold down a lovely job, cooking at this country house with beautiful grounds. It was one with walled gardens – so few of them are still left in the country. There, they grew the most wonderful fruits, veggies, and such white peaches. All of them so fresh and heavenly.

Post Script

Bullies are a certain type of individual, who thrive on what they do to others, numb to normal life's values.

To cope with these people takes courage, and sometimes we haven't the courage, nor are able to confront them. On the other hand, no one needs to know. We don't have the courage, then can put a front on – this is hard and draining on body and soul.

One thing which gives the bullies a fright is to talk about what they have said or done; tell, this is the key to defeat and the route is to tell.

Tell anyone and everyone as many times as possible. This is their 'Achilles heel' – to talk, it dilutes the poison, they shrivel to dust with terror. Never keep anything to yourself as far as bullies are concerned.

There is a life beyond what you're living at the present, the world is chockablock full of wonderful people as well as things to do, see and enjoy, which in turn are treasured, nurtured and cherished.

You are of value. Surviving these people is no mean feat in itself, as many do give up. These tragedies affect every sinus of the whole family, siblings, close friends, etc., left with guilt and 'what if' haunts them until the end of their days. Those who must deal with this gruesome aftermath are to be pitied and admired at the same time.

Those who 'brave it out' acquire 'Rock Star Status' and are known as 'Solid' using an American phrase, leading to being much admired as to what you have come through.

Many of those bullied have landed up with high powered jobs, and turn out to be a credit to the country and whole community.

Winston Churchill's life was a beacon – he battled the bullies at his school, and also coped with depression; he never gave up, he beat them into the ground, and now is the most admired Briton to date.

You are a light: it burns bright, it must never go out. Because of these people, you are able to give to the world everything which these horrors can't. They live in a dark place; you live can live in the light, bring warmth and comfort into lives of others.

To experience this road travelled is to 'toughen the steel' – nothing shall beat you now, just nothing.